D0842986

Questions and Answers About

THE SALEM WITCH TRIALS

KATE LIGHT

PowerKiDS press.

NEW YORK

GLEN COVE PUBLIC LIBRARY
4 GLEN COVE AVENUE
GLEN COVE, NEW YORK 11542-2885

Published in 2019 by The Rosen Publishing Group, Inc.
29 East 21st Street, New York, NY 10010

Copyright © 2019 by The Rosen Publishing Group, Inc.

All rights reserved. No part of this book may be reproduced in any form without permission in writing from the publisher, except by a reviewer.

First Edition

Editor: Kate Light
Book Design: Michael Flynn

Photo Credits: Cover, pp. 7, 16 Bettmann/Getty Images; cover, pp. 1, 3–6, 8–12, 14–24, 26–32 (background texture) NuConcept Dezine/Shutterstock.com; pp. 5, 21 Salem Witch Trials Documentary Archive and Transcription Project, University of Virginia, http://salem.lib.virginia.edu; pp. 8–9 littlenySTOCK/Shutterstock.com; p. 11 North Wind Picture Archives; pp. 13 (main), 15, 19 Everett Historical/Shutterstock.com; p. 13 (inset) © Massachusettes Historical Society, Boston, MA, USA/ Bridgeman Images; p. 17 © Maurice Savage/Alamy; pp. 18, 30 courtesy of the Library of Congress; p. 22 Hulton Archive/Getty Images; p. 23 courtesy of the New York Public Library; p. 25 © North Wind Picture Archives/The Image Works; p. 26 Private Collection/Peter Newark American Pictures/Bridgeman Images; p. 27 Stock Montage/Archive Photos/Getty Images; p. 29 © Peabody Essex Museum, Salem, Massachusettes, USA/Bridgeman Images.

Library of Congress Cataloging-in-Publication Data

Names: Light, Kate, author.
Title: Questions and answers about the Salem witch trials / Kate Light.
Description: New York : PowerKids Press, [2019] | Series: Eye on historical
   sources | Includes index.
Identifiers: LCCN 2018006967| ISBN 9781538341230 (library bound) | ISBN
   9781538341247 (pbk.) | ISBN 9781538341254 (6 pack)
Subjects: LCSH: Trials (Witchcraft)–Massachusetts–Salem–History–17th
   century–Juvenile literature. |
   Witchcraft–Massachusetts–Salem–History–17th century–Juvenile
   literature. | Salem (Mass.)–History–Colonial period, ca.
   1600-1775-Juvenile literature.
Classification: LCC KFM2478.8.W5 L54 2018 | DDC 345.744/50288–dc23
LC record available at https://lccn.loc.gov/2018006967

Manufactured in the United States of America

CPSIA Compliance Information: Batch #CS18PK: For Further Information contact Rosen Publishing, New York, New York at 1-800-237-9932

CONTENTS

WELCOME TO SALEM

The Salem witch trials that occurred in Salem Village, Massachusetts, in 1692 are among the darkest moments in American history. The town eventually changed its name to Danvers, but the witch-hunts that took place there are still famous today.

It all began in February 1692 when Samuel Parris's 9-year-old daughter, Betty, and her 11-year-old cousin, Abigail Williams, began acting strangely. Williams lived at the Parris home because her parents had died. One day Parris returned home from work and found the girls twisting themselves into impossible positions, hiding under chairs, sticking out their tongues, and screaming odd words.

Sources from the Past

Maps are useful for historians, especially when they're primary sources. If a map is drawn while someone is exploring a new area, it's a primary source for that exploration. This map isn't a primary source for the Salem witch trials because the trials occurred more than 150 years before it was created. Even though it's not a primary source, do you think this map is helpful for historians researching the Salem witch trials?

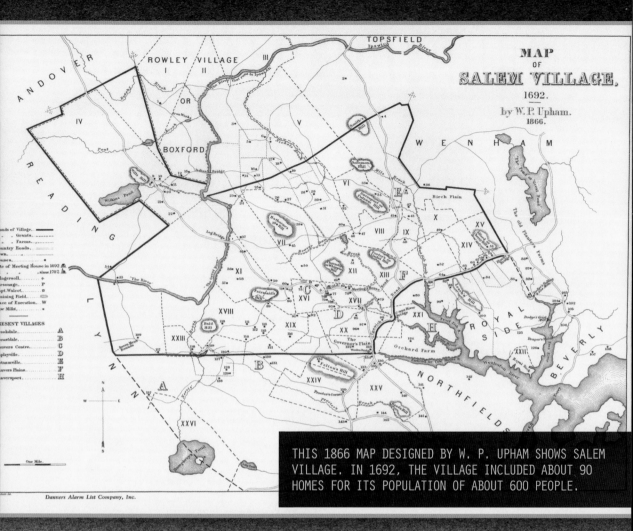

THIS 1866 MAP DESIGNED BY W. P. UPHAM SHOWS SALEM VILLAGE. IN 1692, THE VILLAGE INCLUDED ABOUT 90 HOMES FOR ITS POPULATION OF ABOUT 600 PEOPLE.

There was no natural explanation for this behavior. Parris's doctor, William Griggs, decided the girls were "bewitched." In other words, Dr. Griggs thought the girls were the victims of witchcraft.

PURITAN BELIEFS

Salem was a **Puritan** community. The Puritans had settled in Massachusetts in 1630. Like the **Pilgrims**, they had come to America to practice their religion freely. The Pilgrims wanted to separate from the Church of England, but the Puritans wanted to reform, or change, the teachings of the Church of England. The Puritans set up their own government and laws, just like the Pilgrims.

By 1692, more than 600 people lived in the area of Salem—which included the wealthy Salem Town and Salem Village. The village farmers felt the town was becoming too modern and Puritan values weren't being upheld. The Putnams, a wealthy and powerful family in Salem Village, disliked these changes and established their own church.

ROGER WILLIAMS BECAME THE PASTOR FOR SALEM CHURCH IN 1634, BUT HE WAS SOON FORCED OUT OF MASSACHUSETTS BAY BECAUSE HE BELIEVED IN THE SEPARATION OF CHURCH AND GOVERNMENT. HIS STORY SHOWS THE STRICT PURITAN PRACTICES IN SALEM.

PLAYING WITH MAGIC

Puritan beliefs were very **strict**, and Samuel Parris took his beliefs seriously. By studying various documents, historians have learned that Parris was very interested in the idea of sin and with his own importance. His wife, Elizabeth, was often sick and stuck in bed. Parris's family was often left alone while he was away on church business.

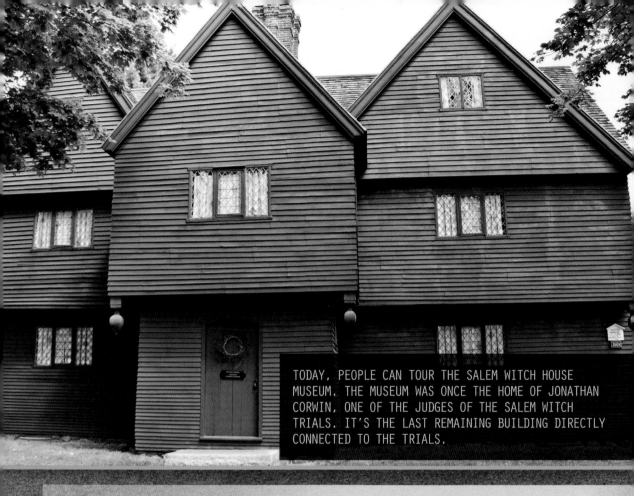

TODAY, PEOPLE CAN TOUR THE SALEM WITCH HOUSE
MUSEUM. THE MUSEUM WAS ONCE THE HOME OF JONATHAN
CORWIN, ONE OF THE JUDGES OF THE SALEM WITCH
TRIALS. IT'S THE LAST REMAINING BUILDING DIRECTLY
CONNECTED TO THE TRIALS.

Possibly to escape this strict lifestyle, Betty Parris and her cousin Abigail Williams would secretly play fortune-telling games with a small group of girls. In one game, the girls would ask questions about the future and then drop an egg white into water to see what shape it took. One February night in 1692, Betty saw a picture relating to death. She began to twist and scream.

ACCUSATIONS

Betty Parris and Abigail Williams blamed their strange behavior on witchcraft. They claimed three women were using magic on them. The accused were Sarah Good, Sarah Osbourne, and a slave named Tituba. Sarah Good was a beggar. Sarah Osbourne had a past that the Puritans thought was "questionable." She had married her servant, Alexander Osbourne.

Shortly after Betty and Abigail accused these three women, 13-year-old Ann Putnam Jr., 17-year-old Mary Walcott, and 17-year-old Elizabeth Hubbard also began to act strangely. They started accusing people of witchcraft, too. According to some accounts, these girls formed a special group to tell their futures. Ann became the leader, accusing the most people of witchcraft. By the time the trials ended, she had accused 62 people.

THIS ILLUSTRATION SHOWS TITUBA AND THE GIRLS WHO ACCUSED HER OF WITCHCRAFT.

Sources from the Past

Tituba was Samuel Parris's slave, which made her an easy target for the girls' false accusations. This illustration is not a primary source. It shows how the artist imagined Tituba. The artist made Tituba look scary and much older than she really was. What do you think of this illustration of Tituba?

PARRIS'S POSITION

Samuel Parris was friends with Thomas and Ann Putnam Sr. He was elected minister of the Putnam's new Salem Village church with their help. Parris also gained ownership of the ministry house and surrounding land, which was unusual at the time.

In October 1691, a new Salem Village committee formed. The committee refused to pay the local tax—which paid Parris's salary—and questioned Parris's ownership of the ministry house. Parris and the Putnams feared that Parris would lose his position. Parris began making sermons, or religious speeches, about how evil was taking over Salem Village. Some historians believe Ann Putnam Jr. was encouraged by her parents to continue the witch-hunt. Many of the people Ann and the other girls accused had issues with the Putnams.

THIS IS A PORTRAIT OF REVEREND SAMUEL PARRIS, BETTY PARRIS'S FATHER. THE PUTNAM FAMILY SUPPORTED HIM, BUT HE HAD MANY ENEMIES IN SALEM VILLAGE.

THE FIRST "WITCHES"

In the 1600s, using witchcraft or interacting with the devil was considered a crime. This crime was punishable by hanging. On February 29, 1692, the first three women accused of witchcraft were arrested.

Tituba was Parris's slave. He reportedly beat her into admitting to witchcraft. Her life was spared only because she confessed out of terror. Sarah Good stood trial. In court, one of the accusing girls cried out that Good's specter, or spirit, was stabbing her with a knife. A broken knife was found on the girl, and Good was found guilty. She was hanged on July 19. Sarah Osbourne died in prison on May 10.

Throughout 1692, about 200 more arrests were made. The town was falling into madness.

THIS ENGRAVING FROM AN UNKNOWN ARTIST SHOWS A YOUNG GIRL TWISTING HER BODY IN A TERRIBLE FIT. THE JUDGES THOUGHT THIS WAS PROOF THAT THE GIRL WAS BEING POSSESSED BY THE ACCUSED. THIS WAS ONE OF THE STRANGE FORMS OF PROOF KNOWN AS "SPECTRAL **EVIDENCE**."

THE SPECIAL COURT

In May 1692, Salem's governor William Phips finally stepped in. He set up the Special Court of Oyer and Terminer to handle the witch trials. The court had seven judges, including William Stoughton, who is remembered as being one of the meanest judges of his time.

THIS STONE SEAT IS IN MEMORY OF BRIDGET BISHOP, THE FIRST PERSON HANGED FOR WITCHCRAFT IN SALEM. BISHOP WAS HANGED ON JUNE 10, 1692.

BRIDGET BISHOP
HANGED
JUNE 10, 1692

Before trial, an accused person was "examined." They were questioned and had their body searched for a "witch's mark," which could be anything from a freckle to a birthmark. During the trials, more than 40 people confessed to being witches. Those confessing sometimes accused others. Strangely, those who confessed were often let go, and those who claimed they were innocent, or not guilty, ended up going to jail or being hanged. The trials were terrifying and unfair, using spectral evidence to find innocent people guilty.

JAIL CONDITIONS

Waiting in jail for a trial was a punishment itself. People believed that if witches were chained up, they had less chance of letting their specters out to attack people. The accused people were often placed in ankle-to-neck chains. Even Dorcas Good, Sarah Good's 4-year-old daughter, was chained to the wall. Like her mother, Dorcas had been accused of being a witch.

Sources from the Past

The 1692 **petition** for **bail** is a primary source because it was written at the time of the event. Why is it important for historians to save firsthand accounts of terrible events like the Salem witch trials? What can we learn from sources written by the accused?

IN 1692, SOME OF THE PRISONERS ACCUSED OF WITCHCRAFT WROTE A PETITION FOR BAIL. IN THE PETITION, THE ACCUSED DESCRIBED THE HORRIBLE CONDITIONS IN THE BOSTON JAIL AND ASKED FOR BAIL SO THEY COULD GO HOME TO WAIT FOR THEIR TRIALS.

Once the "witches" were locked up, the town waited to see if the girls' fits would stop. When they didn't, there were more arrests and examinations. After the examinations, which could last three to five days, the accused returned to prison. The prisons were usually far away from Salem Village.

REBECCA NURSE

On March 23, 1692, 71-year-old Rebecca Nurse was arrested for witchcraft. Nurse was the perfect image of Puritan morals. If she was accused, then no one in Salem was safe. According to historians, it's possible that Nurse and her husband were accused because they had a large amount of land and the townspeople were **jealous**. To make matters worse, it was believed that witchcraft was passed from mother to daughter, and Nurse's mother had been accused in the past.

Nurse never confessed to witchcraft. Instead she said, "I am clear. For my life now lies in your hands." Nurse's family immediately tried to get her a **reprieve**. Governor Phips granted one, but the accusers once again had fits. The community decided that meant Nurse was guilty, and she was hanged on July 19.

THIS IS A PAGE FROM THE COURT
RECORDS OF REBECCA NURSE'S CASE.

Sources from the Past

Historians have saved many official court documents that were written to record the Salem witch trials. There are even records of Rebecca Nurse's "examination," in which Abigail Williams and others accused her of witchcraft. Official documents such as the records of Nurse's case are primary sources. Do you think official records are more trustworthy primary sources than personal accounts such as diary entries? Why or why not?

RISING DOUBTS

The town was very upset about Rebecca Nurse's hanging. People started to have doubts about the witch trials, and many became even angrier with Parris. But as the trials wore on, Parris continued to preach strict Puritan sermons, constantly talking about the need to wash away sin.

THIS ILLUSTRATION SHOWS THE TRIAL OF GILES COREY, AN 80-YEAR-OLD MAN ACCUSED OF WITCHCRAFT. ANN PUTNAM JR. CLAIMED THAT COREY'S SPECTER CAME TO HER ON APRIL 13, 1692, AND ASKED HER TO WRITE IN THE DEVIL'S BOOK. COREY WAS THE ONLY PERSON EXECUTED, OR KILLED, BY BEING CRUSHED TO DEATH.

Soon the girls were not just accusing community **outcasts**—rich and powerful people were called out, too. The accusations began to spin out of control. Mrs. Margaret Thatcher, who was Judge Jonathan Corwin's mother-in-law, was accused of witchcraft. Two sons of the former governor Simon Bradstreet and the wife of Reverend John Hale were also accused. Eventually, in October 1692, the girls accused Lady Phips, the wife of Governor William Phips. However, none of these powerful people were arrested.

SIMON BRADSTREET

THE LEADER OF ALL THE WITCHES

Political issues continued to lead to accusations of witchcraft. This was the case for George Burroughs. He was the minister of Salem Village before Parris and lived with the Putnams for nine months. Through diary accounts, historians have pieced together that there was problems between Burroughs and the Putnams. In 1683, after financial conflicts with the community, Burroughs moved to Maine.

Nine years later, Burroughs was accused of witchcraft and brought back to Salem. Two young women, Abigail Hobbs and Mercy Lewis, claimed that Burroughs was not only a wizard, but also the leader of all the witches. When Burroughs was thrown in prison, 32 people signed a petition stating that he was innocent. Unfortunately, Burroughs was still hanged on August 19, 1692.

THIS ILLUSTRATION SHOWS GEORGE BURROUGHS JUST BEFORE HE WAS HANGED FOR WITCHCRAFT. ONE PIECE OF EVIDENCE USED AGAINST BURROUGHS WAS THE PRESENCE OF TOADS IN HIS NEW HOME. TOADS WERE CONSIDERED THE DEVIL'S CREATURES. THIS TYPE OF "PROOF" LEAD TO BURROUGHS'S WRONGFUL EXECUTION.

ENTER THE MATHERS

Increase Mather and his son, Cotton, were well known in the colonies. They made names for themselves by recording major court cases. They were both also ministers. Although they believed in witchcraft, the Mathers were in favor of stopping the executions in Salem. They felt the evidence was not strong enough to prove the accused were guilty.

THIS IS ONE OF THE **PAMPHLETS** WRITTEN BY COTTON MATHER.

The Wonders of the Invisible World.

OBSERVATIONS

As well *Historical* as *Theological*, upon the NATURE, the NUMBER, and the OPERATIONS of the

DEVILS.

Accompany'd with,

I. Some Accounts of the Grievous Molestations, by DÆMONS and WITCHCRAFTS, which have lately annoy'd the Countrey; and the Trials of some eminent *Malefactors* Executed upon occasion thereof: with several Remarkable *Curiosities* therein occurring.

II. Some Counsils, Directing a due Improvement of the terrible things, lately done, by the Unusual & Amazing Range of EVIL SPIRITS, in Our Neighbourhood: & the methods to prevent the *Wrongs* which those *Evil Angels* may intend against all sorts of people among us, especially in Accusations of the Innocent.

III. Some Conjectures upon the great EVENTS, likely to befall, the WORLD in General, and NEW ENGLAND in Particular; as also upon the Advances of the TIME, when we shall see BETTER DAYES.

IV. A short Narrative of a late Outrage committed by a knot of WITCHES in *Swedeland*, very much Resembling, and so far Explaining, *That* under which our parts of *America* have laboured!

V. THE DEVIL DISCOVERED: In a Brief Discourse upon those TEMPTATIONS, which are the more Ordinary *Devices* of the Wicked One.

By Cotton Mather.

Boston Printed by Benj. Harris for Sam, Phillips. 1693.

Sources from the Past

The Mathers wrote many pamphlets discussing devils and witchcraft. They became famous for their sermons and writings on these subjects. Primary sources like this pamphlet help historians understand what people believed in during the late 1600s. If belief in witchcraft was common, why do you think Salem Village had such an unusually high number of accusations?

COTTON MATHER

In 1693, Increase wrote a famous article based on a sermon he gave in 1692. He wrote, "It were better that ten suspected witches should escape, than one innocent person should be condemned." This meant it would be better to let 10 people believed of being witches go than to hang one person who was innocent. Increase's sermon made people doubt the strange and unfair "evidence" being used in trials.

THE BEGINNING OF THE END

A letter by Thomas Brattle, a wealthy scientist, finally pushed Governor Phips to take action. The letter was dated October 8, 1692. In it, Brattle questioned the witch trials. He didn't understand how spectral evidence could be used in court. One of Brattle's strongest points was that some of the people the girls accused had never even met the girls.

Brattle's letter included a list of well-known men in England who agreed with his points and wanted the trials to stop. Not long after Brattle's letter, Governor Phips forbid anyone else accused of witchcraft from being sent to jail. On October 29, 1692, Phips officially ended the Court of the Oyer and Terminer. He started a new court, the Superior Court of Judicature, which did not allow spectral evidence.

THIS 1853 PAINTING BY TOMPKINS HARRISON MATTESON IS TITLED *EXAMINATION OF A WITCH*. IT'S THOUGHT TO SHOW A SCENE FROM THE SALEM WITCH TRIALS. IN THE CENTER OF THE PAINTING, A WOMAN IS BEING SEARCHED FOR THE "DEVIL'S MARK" TO SEE IF SHE IS A WITCH.

LATE APOLOGIES

The Superior Court of Judicature tried 56 people and **convicted** only 3. But everyone tried—even those found guilty—were **pardoned** by Governor Phips by May 1963. At the end of the Salem witch trials, 19 people had been hanged for witchcraft, 5 people had died while in prison, and Giles Corey had been crushed to death.

It was only years later that Parris admitted he might have been wrong to play a part in the trials. He apologized for his actions on November 26, 1694, by reading a statement to the congregation in the meetinghouse. Ann Putnam Jr., who had accused the most people, also regretted her actions later in life. In 1706, a pastor read her apology to the church. None of the other girls publicly apologized or admitted they were wrong.

WILLIAM PHIPS

GLOSSARY

bail: Money given to a court to allow a prisoner to leave jail and return later for trial.

convict: To find or prove guilty of a crime.

evidence: Something that shows that something else is true.

jealous: Feeling or showing an angry desire to have what someone else has.

outcast: Someone who is not accepted by other people.

pamphlet: A short printed publication with no cover or with a paper cover.

pardon: An act of officially saying that someone judged guilty of a crime will be allowed to go free without punishment.

petition: A formal written request to a leader or government regarding a particular cause.

Pilgrims: The people who sailed on the Mayflower in 1620 from England to America in search of freedom to practice their own beliefs.

Puritans: Members of a religious group in England who opposed the traditional Church of England and moved to America during the 17th century.

reprieve: To the delay the punishment of a prisoner.

strict: Absolute, kept with great care.

INDEX

WEBSITES

Due to the changing nature of Internet links, PowerKids Press has developed an online list of websites related to the subject of this book. This site is updated regularly. Please use this link to access the list: www.powerkidslinks.com/eohs/witch